"A person starts to live when he can live outside himself."
— Albert Einstein

Among the mountains I wandered and
saw blue haze and red crag and was amazed;
 On the beach where the long push under the
endless tide maneuvers, I stood silent;
 Under the stars on the prairie watching
the Dipper slant over the horizon's grass,
I was full of thoughts.

—Carl Sandburg

*The bitter sea of life is boundless;
if one but turns around, there's the shore.*
—Chinese Proverb

> Water, water, everywhere,
> and all the boards did shrink;
> Water, water everywhere,
> nor any drop to drink.
> — Samuel Taylor Coleridge

The tide rises, the tide falls,
The twilight darkens, the curlew calls;
Along the sea-sands damp and brown
The traveller hastens toward the town,
And the tide rises, the tide falls.
— Henry Wadsworth Longfellow

Though we travel the world over to find the beautiful, we must carry it with us, or we find it not.
—Ralph Waldo Emerson

> You never enjoy the world aright, till the sea itself floweth in your veins, till you are clothed with the heavens and crowned with the stars.
> —Thomas Traherne

> Let us wander where we will, the universe is built round about us, and we are central still.
> — Henry David Thoreau

Light breaks where no sun shines;
Where no sea runs, the waters of the heart
Push in their tides.
  — Dylan Thomas

Wide sea, that one continuous murmur breeds
Along the pebbled shore of memory!
                          – John Keats

I need an ocean to teach me:
whatever it is that I learn —music or consciousness,
the single wave in the sea, the abyss of my being,
the guttural rasp of my voice, or the blazing
presumption of fishes and navies—
so much is certain: even in sleep, as if
by the trick of a magnet, I spin on the circle
of wave upon wave of the sea, the sea's university.
— Pablo Neruda

design by laura palese

potter style
www.randomhouse.com
isbn 1-4000-8179-3

the sea is
sways
peacefully